Contents

Happy Christmas, everyone

Christmas is celebrated on the 25th of December. It is the birthday of **Jesus Christ**.

In some countries it gets very cold at Christmas.

We Love
CHRISTMAS

Saviour Pirotta

WAYLAND

© Copyright Wayland 2006

Editor: Kirsty Hamilton
Senior Design Manager: Rosamund Saunders
Designer: Elaine Wilkinson

Published in Great Britain in 2006 by Wayland,
an imprint of Hachette Children's Books
Reprinted in 2007 and 2008 by Wayland, an imprint of
Hachette Children's Books

British Library Cataloguing in Publication Data:
Pirotta, Saviour
We love Christmas
1. Christmas - Juvenile literature
I. Title
394.2'663

ISBN 13: 978 0 7502 4835 8

Printed in China

Wayland
An imprint of Hachette Children's Books
338 Euston Road, London NW1 3BH

The publishers would like to thank the following for
allowing us to reproduce their pictures in this book:

Corbis: 5, Ariel Skelley; 6, Sandro Vanini, Ottaviano di
Martino Nelli; 8, David Mercado; 10, Pagani Flavio, Corbis
Sygma; 12, Adam Woolfitt; 13, Ted Spiegel; 15, Lucy
Pemoni; 16, 18, Becky Lulgart-Stayner; 19, Joseph Sohm;
20, Mary Ellen Bartley; 21, Reuters; 22, Archivo
Iconografico, S.A; 23, Richard Cummins / Getty Images:
title page, 4, Mike Brinson, The Image Bank; cover, 14,
Ray Kachatorian, Taxi; 17, Mel Yates, Stone / Alamy: 9,
Profimedia.CZ s.r.o / Wayland picture library: 7, 11.

Christians and many other people celebrate Christmas with great happiness and give each other presents.

Families get together to celebrate.

5

Away in a manger

Christians believe Jesus is the son of God. During his life on Earth, he taught people how to live better lives and how to love God and one another.

It is said that a cow and a donkey kept baby Jesus warm with their breath.

Children act out the story of Jesus's birth, called the **nativity**.

Jesus was born in a **stable** in the little town of Bethlehem some two thousand years ago.

Deck the halls

Christians call the weeks before Christmas **Advent**. In churches and homes, statues of Jesus and his parents are placed in cribs. They are surrounded by figures of sheep, **shepherds** and **angels**.

Children in Bolivia collect small figures to put in their cribs.

Before Christmas, there is special food to buy, cards to send, decorations to put up and presents to wrap.

Germans light a special candle every sunday during Advent.

Oh Christmas tree, oh Christmas tree

The tree is the most popular Christmas decoration in the world. A long time ago people made their own decorations to put on it.

In Sweden, people decorate the trees in their garden too.

DID YOU KNOW?

Before electricity, people used little candles instead of fairy lights.

Nowadays we buy our decorations from the shops. There are lots to choose from!

Wreaths with bows, holly and mistletoe are hung up.

Peace on Earth

Knock! Knock! On Christmas Eve carol-singers might come to your door to sing you a carol.

Carol singers like these sing songs about the birth of Jesus and what it means to Christians.

It's fun going to church at night when usually you are in bed.

Carols are special songs we sing at Christmas. They are sung in church too, especially at **midnight mass** or service.

Down the chimney

Christmas is a time for sharing. People send each other cards and exchange gifts. Children wait for Father Christmas to bring them presents.

What will you find in your stocking on Christmas morning?

Saint Nicholas was a holy man who liked to help poor people. He was the first Father Christmas.

In Italy, children who have been naughty only get a lump of coal in their stocking.

In Hawaii, Father Christmas travels on a boat.

15

Christmas is a treat

All over the world, people celebrate Christmas with a magnificent feast. In some countries, like England and America, they serve roast turkey.

Russians eat roast goose like this one, or roast pork for Christmas.

DID YOU KNOW?

In Sweden, children enjoy a special Christmas Eve dinner with fish and ham.

Brazilians like to have coloured rice with their turkey. Italians follow it with a slice of special cake called panettone.

At Christmas dinner, crackers are pulled and party hats are worn.

17

Boxing Day

Some say that the day after Christmas is called Boxing Day because it was the day when rich people gave their **servants** a present. It came in a box.

Today, people eat Christmas Day leftovers, like these turkey rolls, on Boxing Day.

DID YOU KNOW?

Some people put coins in Christmas or plum pudding to bring good luck!

Others insist that money from the collection boxes in churches was given to the poor.

This man is helping the poor by preparing free Christmas meals for **homeless** people.

A happy New Year

In a lot of countries, celebrating the new year has become a part of Christmas. Parties are organised so that people can wish each other all the best for the year ahead.

Portuguese children eat twelve grapes as the clock strikes the New Year.

DID YOU KNOW?

On New Year's Eve, Italians throw their old furniture out of the window. 'Out with the old and in with the new!' they say.

Happy New Year!

We three kings

In many countries the 6th of January is a great celebration. People remember the day when the three kings brought their gifts to Jesus. Some call it 'Epiphany'. Others know it as 'The Day of the Kings'.

The three kings brought gifts of gold, **frankincense** and myrrh.

The next day many people start putting away the decorations. Christmas is over. But we'll celebrate it again next year.

In Mexico, children break open a **piñata** like this one, at Epiphany, to get sweets and money.

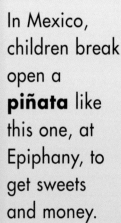

Index and glossary

Advent the four weeks leading up to Christmas
angels messengers from God
frankincense / myrrh types of tree gum that make a sweet
   smell when burnt
homeless when a person has nowhere to live
Jesus Christ the person who started the Christian religion
midnight mass a church service held on Christmas Eve at midnight
nativity the story of the birth of Jesus Christ
piñata a cardboard figure that Mexicans break open to find sweets
   and money
servants people who cook and clean for someone else
shepherd a person who looks after sheep
stable a building where horses are kept